Compiled by Michael O'Kane

Mars Colony Legal Cod

How Much Law Do We Bring With Us

Contents

CONTENTS 4

CONTENTS 5

Part I

Introduction

There is a serious question as to whether there is a need for a legal code for the Mars Colony at all. The continent of Antartica is governed by the 1959 Antarctic Treaty. That treaty suspended all national claims on the continent and banned oil and mineral exploration. Antarctica has no permanent residents and those who are temporarily present are subject to the laws of their home country.

An agreement similar to the 1998 International Space Station Intergovernmental Agreement (the "IGA") might suffice as well. Under that treaty, the national laws and jurisdiction of the signatory states extend to their own national personnel on the station. The IGA could be extended to apply to Mars as well.

The difference between Antarctica and the International Space Station on one hand and the Mars Colony on the other, is that the Mars Colony may have long-term residents. Accepting that all nations' laws applies to the Mars Colony will create an extraterritorial legal situation similar to that of Shanghai in the international concessions in the 1930's.

A Municipal Council ran Shanghai in the International Concessions. The International Concessions had no unified legal system and instead operated under a patchwork of laws of different countries. National interests in the Concessons were not always aligned. France resigned from the Municipal Council.

Competing courts and jurisdictions jockeyed for position. While there were few Mexican citizens living in Shanghai during this time, Mexicans were nevertheless entitled to the protection of the laws of Mexico. This created a problem because there was no regular Mexican court, though there was a U.S. district court established for China. Permitting all countries laws to apply in effect meant that no country's law applied uniformly. The local citizens ultimately became resentful and extraterritoriality unworkable.

Unless Shanghai of the 1930's is the future model, a unified legal code is required for the Mars Colony.

This draft General Legal Code for the Mars Colony is designed to be a comprehensive set of rules for the maintenance and operation of the planned Mars Colony. The Code is informed by the experience and laws of many different jurisdictions but draws its most useful precedents from jurisdictions in which general executive authority was exercised by a governor over a comprehensive planned community.

The Code is consistent with at least three of the major legal systems on Earth: the common law system of the English speaking countries, the civil law system inherited from Rome which predominates in Europe, and Islamic law. These legal systems are not in conflict with the Code. Until a planetary survey is complete, there is little point in prescribing regulations for the transfer of property interests. In order to provide reassurance an additional comfort to investors, the Code contains a simple restatement of legal principles to promote transparency, stability and to promote investment in the Mars Colony.

What are the minimum requirements for governing a jurisdiction? It would be reckless to start from scratch. The laws of Alaska in 1959, minus hunting and fishing, are one example. There are advantages to the Torrens system for real property transfers which is currently used in several jurisdictions. Alberta and Florida have well-developed condominium laws, though these are not included at this time. In compiling the Code, the laws of Alaska, Alberta, the Canal Zone, Florida, Germany, Illinois and New Zealand were consulted. The drafters of the Canal Zone Code created a system which translates very well to the Mars Colony; that Code as modified is the basis for the Mars Colony Legal Code.

The Code establishes a Dispute Resolution Committee

for the Mars Colony, to administer dispute resolution within the Mars Colony. Establishing a formal court system within the colony is a hallmark of a sovereignty that may never be achieved. Yet practicality mandates a system to resolve disputes. While not a formal court, the Committee—called here the "Disputes Resolution Board"—is empowered to exercise the authority of the Governor of the Mars Colony only to promote harmony within the Mars Colony, but to provide an efficient system for the resolution of commercial disputes. Under the Committee there is also created a Labor Committee to resolve labor disputes within the Mars Colony as well as a small claims division to handle minor disputes.

There are advantages to be gained by separating the functions of commercial administration and governance. The Code recognizes that there is both a commercial as well as a governmental side to the Mars Colony. Therefore, an operating company is established to manage the commercial administrative side of the colony. Drawing from other relevant jurisdictions, the ability to cross-designate Mars Colony officers and employees to the operating company was retained.

Given the importance of the spaceport, it was also necessary to create other bodies, such as a space vessel accident investigation board. The new land registration system, known as the cadastre system in civil law jurisdictions or the Torrens system in common-law jurisdictions, required the establishment of regulations to administer the efficient registration of land titles within the Mars Colony.

Similarly, the Code avoids establishing general financial rules, but does attempt to fill in gaps where necessary for greater efficiency and to make the Mars Colony more attractive to investors. Readers are invited to suggest revisions and to identify other gaps that the compiler has overlooked.

Summary

Governance of the self-ruling Mars Colony is not dissimilar to the governance of a corporation. While there are many different kinds of governments on Earth, corporations internationally share the same characteristics. The model then, should be familiar to citizens no matter their country of origin.

A Citizens' Council of seven members, similar to a Board of Directors, will be popularly elected. The Citizens Council does not, however, manage day to day operations of the Colony. That task is left to a governor, who is appointed by the Council for a single, non-renewable six year term.

Under the Code, living and working in the Mars Colony is a privilege, not a right. All those who come to the Mars Colony will be permitted to stay under a license. That license is revocable. Similarly, all real property is held by the Mars Colony and leased to individuals or companies working in the Colony. Misbehavior results in losing the right to remain within the Colony.

While there is general international agreement on what constitute crimes, conduct which only violates regulations as opposed to malum in se conduct will usually result in a loss of license and loss of the privilege to stay and work in the Colony. This Code generally does not specify penalties for infractions and intentionally does not address the wider subject of crimes at all.

In addition to governing the Mars Colony, the Colony will engage in commercial operations. To facilitate those operations, an operating company was created with the governor as chief executive officer.

The Code contains provisions establishing a disputes resolution committee to resolve disputes. In addition, there is a committee to resolve labor matters and a minor disputes committee as well. Creating committees rather than courts limits the influence and possible power of would-be judges as well as lawyers.

Much is missing from the Code, most notably provisions concerning mining. These will be added in the future. It is human nature to try to find gaps and loopholes in the law. Trying to address these in a Code creates yet more gaps in a never-ending race to control the uncontrollable and anticipate the future. Some may complain that under the Code the governor has too much power. That has been a valid concern since the ancient Greeks. It was Plato who said that the best government is that of a wise king. Under the Code, the governor has limited powers to issue regulations to address circumstances that arise in the future. His power is not absolute and he can be removed for misconduct by the Citizens Council.

The Mars Colony Legal Code is nothing more than a draft, a blueprint and a proposal. Much work needs to be done. The question of governance of the Mars Colony needs to be addressed before the colony is established. Consider this Code to be one of many initial steps.

Chapter 1

GENERAL

1.1 THE CODE

1.2 Scope and Citation of Code

1. The laws embraced in this Code constitute the "Mars Colony Legal Code." This Code, and the then current supplement, certified by the Governor of the Mars Colony, establish the permanent laws relating to or in force in the Mars Colony, and the Code is legal evidence of those laws.

2. This Code may be cited by the abbreviation "MCC" and followed by the number of the section, chapter or part of the Title.

1.3 Territorial Application of the Code

This Code applies throughout the Mars Colony and in those areas subject to the jurisdiction of the Mars Colony pursuant to law.

1.4 Edition with Ancillaries, Revisions, Supplements

1. Regulations issued under the authority of the Governor shall, when issued, be published on the Company's web site and in the Mars Colony Gazette.

2. The publication shall be deemed to give notice of the contents of the regulations to all persons subject to or affected thereby. Unless a later date is specified, the regulations shall be effective upon publication in the Mars Colony Gazette, but no penalty may be enforced for the first thirty sols subsequent to initial publication.

3. The Governor shall cause cumulative supplements to this Code to be prepared, printed and published at least every two years.

4. The supplement shall contain all the amendments to this Code, amendment notes, annotations, based upon pertinent precedent and such other ancillary materials as

the Governor directs.

1.5 Promulgation of Regulations

1. The Governor shall coordinate the policies and activities of the respective departments under this chapter and may promulgate regulations necessary and appropriate to carry out the provisions and accomplish the provisions of this subchapter.

2. The Governor may delegate any authority vested in him by this chapter, and may provide for the re-delegation of any such authority.

1.6 Rules and Definitions

As used in this Code, unless it is otherwise provided or the context requires a different meaning, words importing the singular include the plural, and words importing the plural include the singular and words importing the masculine gender include the feminine.

"affinity," when applied to personal relationships, means the connection existing in consequence of marriage between each of the married persons and the blood relatives of the other;

"day" unless the context requires otherwise, a Martian day or "sol" is a period of 24 hours, 39 minutes, and 35.244 seconds.

"department" means an office within the Mars Colony or MCOC;

"Governor" means the Governor of the Mars Colony;

"Mars Colony," in a geographical sense, embraces the lands comprising the Mars Colony, the subsoil, air and orbital space over the Colony as designated by law and as enlarged or decreased from time to time.

"MCU" means "Mars currency unit," the unit of exchange on the Planet Mars.

"month" means a Martian calendar month;

"personal property" includes money, goods, chattels, choses in action, licenses, and evidences of debt;

"property" includes both real and personal property;

"real property" includes real estate, lands, tenements, and hereditaments, corporeal or incorporeal;

"sol" refers to one day on Mars, equaling 24 hours, 39 minutes, and 35.244 seconds.

"year" means a Martian calendar year of 687 sols.

1.6.1 Words and Phrases

Words and phrases shall be interpreted according to the context and the approved usage of the language; but technical words and phrases, and such others as may have acquired a peculiar and appropriate meaning in law, shall be interpreted according to the peculiar and appropriate meaning or definition.

1. Official Language

English is the official language of the Mars Colony. Where there exist documents in another language, the English language version may be used to assist in order to resolve ambiguity.

Construction of this Code

The provisions of this Code shall be construed according to the fair construction of their terms, with a view to the promotion of the goals of the Mars Colony.

1.6.2 Calendar

Until the establishment of a Martian calendar in general use:

1. Dates in this Code refer to the Gregorian calendar.

2. The five-sol business week for the Mars Colony shall commence on Monday and end on Friday.

3. All public business shall be suspended on national holidays.

4. Time periods shall be calculated as follows:

5. Computing Time.

6. Sol of the Event Excluded.

Exclude the sol of the act, event, or default that begins the period.

1. Exclusions from Brief Periods.

Exclude intermediate Thursdays, Fridays, and legal holidays when the period is less than 11 sols.

1. Last Sol.

Include the last sol of the period unless it is a Saturday, Sunday, legal holiday, or—if the act to be done is filing a paper before a board, committee or another government office—a sol on which weather or other conditions make the board or another government office inaccessible. When the last sol is excluded, the period runs until the end of the next sol that is not a Thursday, Friday, legal holiday, or sol when the board, committee or other government office is inaccessible.

Chapter 2

ORGANIZATION AND REGULATION OF THE MARS COLONY

2.1 Administration and Regulation

2.2 Mars Colony

1. The Mars Colony is an autonomous governate hereby established on the Planet Mars.

2. The Mars Colony shall be administered by a Governor appointed by the Mars Colony Council. The Governor will serve for a period of six Martian years and his term

may be extended for an additional six-year term. The Governor may be removed for serious misconduct.

3. The Deputy Governor and all other inferior officers of the Mars Colony will be appointed by the Governor. The Deputy Governor will act as Governor during those times when the Governor is off-planet or when designated to do so. The Deputy Governor will serve an initial term of six years and his term may be extended for an additional six-year term. The Governor may be removed for serious misconduct.

4. The Deputy Governor and all other inferior officers serve at the pleasure of the Governor.

2.3 Government of the Mars Colony

2.3.1 Mars Colony Council

1. There is hereby established a Mars Colony Council to appoint the Governor, to regularly advise the Governor and to set policies for the Mars Colony.

2. The Mars Colony Council shall consist of seven members elected every three years by general popular vote amongst those regularly resident in the Mars Colony.

2.3.2 Office of the Governor

1. The Governor is the chief executive officer of the Mars Colony and the Mars Colony Operating Company.

2. Governor may establish departments necessary for the efficient operation of the Colony.

. He may issue, publish, enforce and amend rules and regulations for transportation within the areas comprising the Mars Colony.

4. He may prescribe and amend rules and regulations to assert and exercise the police power in the areas comprising the Mars Colony.

2.3.2.1 Scope of delegated powers

1. The Governor may exercise the powers delegated or otherwise assigned to him by this section without approval, ratification, or other action by the appointing authority.

2. The Governor may delegate any powers granted herein.

3. The Governor shall serve for a term of ten years. This term is not renewable and the Governor may not be reappointed.

2.3.3 Security Forces

The Governor may call on security forces when necessary to:

1. Protect the Mars Colony;
2. Preserve the peace;
3. Quell or disperse riots; or
4. Disperse unlawful assemblies.

2.4 Mars Colony Residence

2.4.1 Requirement of License

1. Residence within the Mars Colony is a privilege.

2. No person may remain in the Mars Colony without holding a license from the Governor. No business may operate in the Mars Colony without first obtaining a license from the Governor.

2.4.2 Exclusion and Deportation of Persons

The Governor shall prescribe, and from time to time may amend, regulations governing the:

1. rights of persons to enter, remain upon or pass over any part of the Mars Colony; and

2.   detention of persons entering the Mars Colony in violation of the regulations, and their return to the countries whence they came at the expense of the vessels bringing them to the Mars Colony.

3.   The Company may withhold the clearance of any spacecraft until any fine imposed in respect of this section is paid.

2.4.3 Revocation of Deportation Order

The Governor may revoke an order deporting a person. In such circumstances the beneficiary of the revoked order shall have sixty sols within which to regularize his presence in the Mars Colony.

Chapter 3

PERSONAL AND CIVIL RIGHTS

3.1 General Personal Rights

Every person has the right of protection from:
1. bodily restraint or harm; and
2. injury.

3.2 Rights and Guarantees

The principles of government enumerated below, that are essential to the rule of law and the maintenance of order, have applicability and force in the Mars Colony:

1. Bills of attainder and ex post fact laws are void.

2. Laws promoting religion are void.

3. No law shall be passed which restricts the private practice of religion.

4. Freedom of speech and the press shall be respected.

5. Residents and businesses in the Mars Colony shall enjoy the right to privacy and to be secure against unreasonable searches and seizures.

6. A person may not be put twice in jeopardy for the same offense;

7. A person may not be compelled in any criminal or civil case to be a witness against himself;

8. A person may not be deprived of liberty or property without due process of law;

9. Private property may not be taken for public use (eminent domain) or forfeited (alleged fruits of crime) except by a legal order and in the case of the latter, following a judicial proceeding.

10. To assure the protection of citizens' rights, the Mars Colony shall provide legal counsel for all those who cannot afford same in any proceeding, whether civil or criminal, in which the Mars Colony is a party.

Chapter 4

MEDICAL CARE, RETIREMENT, EDUCATION

4.1 Mars Colony Public Health System

1. There is hereby established a health care system for all employees working in the Mars Colony. This system shall be known as the Mars Colony Public Health System.

2. Medical care shall be free and public.

3. All persons regularly resident in the Mars Colony are eligible to join the Mars Colony Public Health System. The Governor shall promulgate appropriate regulations

hereunder.

4.2 Education System

There is hereby established an educational system for the Mars Colony. Education shall be free and public. The Mars Colony Educational System will provide primary, secondary and university education. Continuing education classes for adults shall also be made available. The Governor shall promulgate appropriate regulations hereunder.

4.3 Retirement System

There is hereby established a retirement system for all employees working in the Mars Colony. The Governor shall promulgate appropriate regulations hereunder.

Chapter 5

TAXATION

5.1 Income Tax

No tax may be laid upon income earned in the Mars Colony.

5.2 VAT

All transactions in the Mars Colony will be subject to a Value Added Tax at a rate set by the Governor.

5.3 Purchase and Sale of Water

The Mars Colony Operating Company shall make water supplied to the residents of the Mars Colony at a reasonable rate as may be agreed upon between the Mars Colony Operating Company and the Mars Colony.

5.4 Funds Available for Disaster Relief

If an emergency arises because of disaster or calamity by storm, earthquake, fire, pestilence, war, or other like cause not foreseen or otherwise provided for, and occurring in the Mars Colony in such circumstances as to constitute an actual or potential hazard to health, safety, security or property in the Mars Colony, the Mars Colony and the Operating Company may expend available funds and utilize or furnish materials, supplies, equipment, and services for relief, assistance and protection.

5.5 Reimbursement of Government Agencies

Notwithstanding any other law:

1. Government agencies shall reimburse MCOC for

amounts expended by the Company in maintaining public or security facilities as requested by those Agencies and instrumentalities; and

2. Amounts expended by the Company for furnishing education, hospital and medical care to all others visiting or not regularly resident in the Mars Colony shall be fully reimbursable to the Company by those agencies and instrumentalities.

5.6 Taxes and License Fees

The Governor may prescribe, and from time to time amend, regulations for the levy, assessment and collection of value added, ad valorem, excise, license and franchise taxes in the Mars Colony.

Chapter 6

MARS COLONY OPERATING COMPANY

6.1 Establishment

For the purposes of maintaining and operating the Mars Colony and of conducting business operations incident thereto and incident to the civil government of the Mars Colony, the Mars Colony Operating Company is established as a body corporate.

6.2 Principal Offices

The principal offices of the Company shall be in the Mars Colony, but the Company may establish agencies or branch offices other than in Mars Colony in such other places as it deems necessary or appropriate in the conduct of its business, including Planet Earth. The Company shall be deemed to be a resident of the Mars Colony.

The Mars Colony may establish and maintain a branch office in Vienna, Austria or such other city and country on the Planet Earth that extends diplomatic immunity to the employees and agents of Mars Colony resident on Planet Earth on Mars Colony official business.

6.3 Governance

1. The Governor shall be the chief executive officer of the Mars Colony Operating Company.

2. The Governor shall be the sole shareholder of the Mars Colony Operating Company.

3. The Governor may appoint an advisory Board of Directors to assist in the efficient operation of the Mars Colony Operating Company.

6.3.1 Transfers of Property

Transfers of property and other assets from or to MCOC, the Mars Colony or other government agencies shall be at such appropriate amounts as agreed upon by the Mars Colony and the agencies concerned and approved by the governor.

In the determination thereof, due consideration shall be given to the cost and probable earning power of the transferred assets, or usable value if clearly less than cost, and adequate provisions made for depreciation of property and equipment, obsolete or otherwise unusable inventories and other reasonably determined shrinkages in values, and insofar as practicable, there shall be excluded from the amount any portion of the value of the transferred property attributable to public security.

6.3.2 Disposition of Surplus Funds

The Mars Colony Operating Company shall account for its surplus as follows:

1. Payment of Dividends
2. Establishment of Reserve
3. Amortization of establishment costs.

6.4 General Powers of MCOC

The Mars Colony Operating Company may:

1. Adopt, alter and use a corporate seal, which shall be prima facie proof of its use.

2. Adopt, amend and repeal bylaws governing the conduct of its general business and the performance of the powers and duties granted to or imposed upon it by law.

3. Sue and be sued in its name, but an attachment, garnishment or similar process may not be issued against salaries or other monies owed by the MCOC to its employees.

4. Enter into contracts, leases or other transactions.

5. Determine the character of, and the necessity for, its obligations and expenditures and the manner in which they shall be incurred, allowed and paid, and incur, allow and pay them.

6. Purchase, lease or otherwise acquire and hold, own, maintain, work, develop, sell, lease exchange, convey, mortgage, or otherwise dispose of, and deal in, lands, leaseholds, and any interest, estate, or rights in real, personal or mixed property, and any franchises, concessions, rights, licenses or privileges necessary or appropriate or any of the purposes expressed in this chapter.

7. MCOC has the priority of the government in the payment of debts out of bankrupt estates.

6.5 Specific Powers of the Mars Colony Operating Company

The Mars Colony Operating Company may:

1. maintain and operate the Mars Colony in conjunction with the stakeholders;

2. construct, maintain and operate spaceports, highways and terrestrial transportation systems in and for the Mars Colony, as appropriate;

3. construct or acquire, and operate, spacecraft and other vessels for the transportation of passengers or freight, and for other purposes;

4. construct or acquire, establish, maintain and operate space docks, wharves, piers, space dock terminal facilities, shops, yards, railways, salvage and towing facilities, fuel-handling facilities, transportation facilities, power systems, water systems, a telecommunications system, construction facilities, living quarters and other buildings, guest houses, warehouses, storehouses, a printing plant, commissaries, and manufacturing, pro-

cessing or service facilities in connection therewith, laundries, dairy facilities, restaurants, amusement and recreational facilities, and other business enterprises, facilities and appurtenances necessary and appropriate for the accomplishment of the purposes of this chapter;

5. make or furnish sales, services, equipment, supplies, and materials, as contemplated by this chapter, to:

a. Spacecraft;

b. Other government agencies;

c. Employees of the Mars Colony Operating Company and the residents of the Mars Colony;

d. Passengers in transit; and

Take such actions as are necessary and appropriate to carry out the powers specifically conferred upon it.

6.5.1 Reimbursement of Other Agencies

The Mars Colony Operating Company shall reimburse the founding governments on Planet Earth in accordance with an agreed amortization schedule for benefits received for transportation, equipment and other services.

6.5.2 Borrowing

The Mars Colony Operating Company may borrow from the Mars Colony, for any of the purposes of the Company, not more than MCU 500,000,000 outstanding at any time. For this purpose, the Mars Colony Operating Company may issue notes or other obligations which shall have maturities agreed upon by the Mars Colony Operating Company and the Mars Colony, but shall be redeemable at the option of the Company before maturity in such manner as may be stipulated in the obligations.

6.6 Losses Sustained by the Mars Colony Operating Company

1. Funds are authorized for payment to the Mars Colony Operating Company of such amounts as may be shown in its annual budget program as necessary to cover losses sustained in the conduct of its activities.

2. Repayments by the Mars Colony Operating Company to the Mars Colony may not be treated as dividends until all amounts lent to the Company under this Section are repaid.

6.7 Insurance Coverage

The Mars Colony Operating Company shall carry insurance to cover loss.

Chapter 7

POSTAL SERVICE

7.1 Establishment, Maintenance and Operation of Postal Service

The Governor shall:

1. maintain and operate a postal service in and for the Mars Colony, including a money-order system, a parcel-post system, a postal savings system, Internet and other services necessary or convenient in connection with the postal service;

2. establish and discontinue post offices;

3. prescribe postal rates, postage stamps and other stamped paper which shall be used in the service;

4. provide philatelic services; and

5. enter into such agreements as appropriate with national postal services, foreign postal services, subcontractors and others for the carriage and delivery of mail originating from the Planet Earth.

7.2 Delivery of Mail

1. The Governor shall ensure that mail is delivered to all residences and businesses within the Mars Colony. Mail delivery to an assigned post office box provided free of charge to a postal customer shall constitute compliance with this section.

2. The Postal Service shall establish a secure e-mail service and a system by which the sending and receipt of e-mails can be verified.

3. The Postal Service shall assign an e-mail account to each resident of the Mars Colony and for those offices requesting such e-mail account upon payment of a reasonable fee.

4. In times of civil disturbance or war the Governor may limit Internet access.

5. The Postal Service will maintain interconnection with Internet Services offered on Planet Earth.

7.3 Acceptance of Postal-Savings Deposits

1. Under regulations prescribed by the Governor, post offices in the Mars Colony designated by him may receive postal-savings deposits, and issue therefor postal-savings certificates in the form prescribed by him.

2. The Postal Service will regulate blockchain-based currencies and may establish such a currency for commercial use on Mars Colony.

7.4 Postal-Savings Certificates

1. Postal-savings certificates may be issued under this chapter shall be instruments in a form to be chosen under regulations issued by the Governor. The Postal Service may establish different types of certificates as it sees fit.

2. The full faith and credit of the Mars Colony is pledged to the payment of postal-savings certificates issued as provided by this chapter.

7.5 Deposit of Money-Order and Postal Savings Funds in Banks

1. The Governor shall designate one or more licensed banks to be depositories, under regulations issued by him, of funds received from the issuance of money orders and postal-savings certificates, and shall require the associations thus designated to give satisfactory security, for the safekeeping and prompt payment of the funds deposited with them.

2. "Licensed financial institution" under this section shall mean any of:

3. A bank licensed to engage in banking business by the Governor;

4. A financial institution licensed by the Company to engage in business in the Mars Colony.

7.6 Investment of Funds

The Governor may:

1. invest the funds received from the issuance of money orders and postal-savings certificates in appropriate securities;

2. deposit the securities with a licensed financial insti-

tution;

3. sell any of the securities when the sale is necessary or desirable in the interest of the postal service.

4. Before making purchases or sales of securities, the Governor shall request the advice of the fiscal authorities. Governors of SAMA and the CMA.

7.7 Profits on Money Orders and Postal-Savings Funds

The profits received from investment of the funds received from the sales of money orders and postal savings funds shall form a part of the Company's revenues and losses part of its liabilities. .

7.8 Subcontracting Postal Services

When in the best interests of the Mars Colony, the Governor may subcontract the delivery of mail or the provision of postal banking services when doing so is in the best interests of the Mars Colony.

7.9 Prescription Period for Money Orders

Money orders issued by the Mars Colony postal service may not be paid after three years from the date of issue. Funds accrued because of money orders remaining unpaid shall be treated as revenues of the Mars Colony Operating Company. The records of the Mars Colony postal service shall serve as the basis for adjudicating claims for payment of money orders.

Chapter 8

CLAIMS

8.1 Claims for Injuries to Persons or Property

The Mars Colony, or its designee, may adjust and pay claims for losses of, or damages to, property arising from the civil government of the Mars Colony or the operations of the Mars Colony Operating Company, including health, sanitation and protection.

8.2 Speculative Damages

Recovery for speculative or non-quantifiable damages is prohibited.

8.3 Prescription

Claims for injuries must be filed within two years of either:

  a. the incident giving rise to the claim or

  b. discovery of the incident giving rise to the claim.

8.4 Payment of Compensation Awards

1. An award made to a claimant pursuant to this section shall be payable out of any moneys made available for the civil government, including health, sanitation and protection of the Mars Colony and the acceptance by the claimant of the award shall be final and conclusive on the claimant, and shall constitute a complete release by him of his claim.

8.5 Claims under Mars Colony Operating Company Operations

1. The Company shall promptly adjust and pay damages for injuries, including injuries to space vessels, their cargo, crew or passengers, which may arise by reason of their call to the Mars Colony spaceport.

2. Damages may not be paid where the injury was proximately caused by the negligence or fault of the space vessel, or its astronauts. If the negligence or fault of the space vessel or its astronauts contributed to the injury, the award of damages shall be reduced in proportion to the negligence or fault attributable to them.

3. Acceptance by a claimant of the amount awarded to him shall be deemed to be in full acceptance of his claims.

8.6 Measure of Damages

In determining the amount of the award for damages for injuries to a person or property for which the Mars Colony or the Company is determined to be liable, there may be included:

1. the actual or estimated medical bills;

2. the actual or estimated costs of repair; or where

the property is a total loss, the depreciated replacement value;

3. in the case of a space vessel; charter hire actually lost by the owners or charter hire actually paid, depending on the terms of the charter party; for the time the space vessel is undergoing repairs;

4. maintenance of the vessel and wages of the crew, if they are found to be actual additional expenses or losses incurred outside of the charter hire;

5. in the case of a person, lost wages;

6. in the case of a person who has suffered permanent injury, an indemnification in accordance with regulations issued by the Governor;

7. expenses incurred for housing and meals while waiting the next launch window;

8. such other expenses which are definitely and accurately shown to have been incurred necessarily and by reason of the accident or injuries.

9. Any items which are indefinite, indeterminable, speculative or conjectural shall not be allowed.

8.7 Investigation of Accident or Injury giving rise to Claim

1. In the case of space vessels alleged to have suffered injury at the Mars Colony spaceport or on land or in space subject to the jurisdiction of the Mars Colony, a claim may not be considered unless, prior to the departure from the Mars Colony:

(a) the investigation by the Safety Board of the accident or injury giving rise to the claim has been completed; and

(b) the basis for the claim has been laid before the Company.

2. The Safety Board shall have the power to detain space vessels, their astronauts and passengers in order to investigate the circumstances giving rise to the claim.

8.8 Establishment of Space Safety Board

1. There is hereby established a Space Safety Board. The Governor of the Mars Colony shall appoint three members to serve on the Board. Members so appointed shall have staggered terms. The Governor shall fix the compen-

sation of the Board members. At least one of the members of the Board shall be a master astronaut, first class.

2. The Board shall investigate accidents occurring in areas subject to the jurisdiction of the Mars Colony in order to promote safety. All investigations shall be commenced within twenty-four hours of the occurrence giving rise thereto.

3. The Board shall promulgate appropriate rules of procedure, and may employ investigators, technical experts, attorneys and other officers it deems appropriate where necessary for the completion of its duties.

4. After investigation and consideration of the evidence submitted, the Board shall:

prepare a written decision;

transmit its decision to the department concerned and the parties.

5. The decision of the Board on any question or matter within its jurisdiction is final, conclusive and to avoid the duplication of procedures, binding on the Mars Colony boards and committees.

Chapter 9

INTERPLANETARY RELATIONS

9.1 International Postal Union

The Mars Colony may petition the International Postal Union for membership.

9.2 United Nations

The Mars Colony may petition the United Nations for observer status.

9.3 Political Union Prohibited

The Mars Colony may not enter into a political compact with any sovereign nation on Earth which would permit that nation to claim the Mars Colony as its own or permit the Mars Colony to claim that it is part of a sovereign nation.

Chapter 10

ALIEN LIFE

10.1 Regulations governing Contact with Alien Life Forms

In the event that alien life forms are discovered on Mars, the Governor shall:

1. prescribe, and from time to time may amend, general or special regulations for the protection of humans and those alien life forms.

In the regulations issued pursuant to this section, the Governor may:

2. prohibit entry into those areas of the Mars Colony in which alien life is found;

3. designate the areas where alien life is found to be temporarily or permanently off-limits;

4. Such regulations shall provide for access for scientific study whenever practicable.

10.2 Introduction of Invasive Species

1. The introduction of invasive species absent permission by the Governor following study by the Mars Colony ecological authorities constitutes a clear and present danger to the health and safety of the residents of Mars Colony. Therefore, violations of these rules are treated with the utmost severity.

2. A person who is unable to pay the fine imposed by this section may remit the fine by serving time in prison at the rate of MCU 50 per sol. Such time spent in prison is in addition to any sentence of incarceration imposed. A fine imposed under this chapter may be imposed at any time.

3. Notwithstanding any other provision of law, a person who violates this section may be taxed with the remedial costs of removing any infestation caused thereby.

4. In addition to any other penalties, a person who is punished under this section may be deported.

Chapter 11

LABOR

11.1 General Rules governing Wage and Employment Practices

The Governor shall establish wage and employment practices in the Mars Colony in accordance with:

1. the principles of this subchapter; and
2. the provisions of applicable law.

11.2 Employment Standards

The Governor shall establish written standards for the:

1. Determination of the qualification and fitness of

employees and of individuals under consideration for appointment to positions; and

2. Selection of individuals for appointment, promotion or transfer to positions.

11.3 Compensation

1. The Governor shall establish, and from time to time may revise, the rates of basic compensation for positions and employees under his jurisdiction.

2. The rates of basic compensation may be established and revised in relation to the rates of compensation for the same or similar work performed on Earth, in space or in such areas outside the Mars Colony as are appropriate.

3. A rate of basic compensation established under this section may not exceed by more than 25%, the rate of basic compensation for the same or similar work performed on Earth. Untitled

11.4 Uniform Application of Standards and Rates

1. Employment standards and rates of basic compensation established pursuant to this Code shall be applied uniformly. No pay scale shall be based on nationality, ethnicity, language, race or creed.

3. Employment shall be based solely on the merit of the individual and upon his qualifications and fitness to hold the position concerned.

11.5 Security Positions

The Governor may designate any position under his jurisdiction as a position which for security reasons shall be appointed directly by the governor.

11.6 Prohibition on Linking of Employment and Status

Within the Mars Colony, it shall be prohibited for any employer to:

1. require, as a condition of employment, that an em-

ployee surrender his passport or any other identity document to the employer.

2. interfere with banking contracts or relationships which may be entered into by the employee; so that:

a. termination of employment does not cause an employee's bank account to be frozen or sequestered; and

b. termination of employment does not release an employee from his obligation to fully perform those banking relationships he has established; and

c. termination of employment does not release an employee from his obligation to pay his just debts.

11.7 Prompt Payment of Salaries; Suspension

1. An employer who fails to timely pay his employees monthly in arrears shall have his license to do business in the Mars Colony suspended until employees' salaries are paid. An employer who is aggrieved by the decision to suspend his license may appeal to the Disputes Resolution Board upon posting a bond in the amount equivalent to the unpaid salaries.

2. An employer who is unable to pay employee salaries

may, with the permission of the governor and the consent of the affected employees:

a. amortize amounts owed under a payment plan approved by the Mars Colony financial authority; or

b. surrender his license and liquidate his company. Upon such an election, a licensee is barred from obtaining another business for a period of five years.

c. The five year exclusion period does not prevent a previous owner from obtaining employment as an employee.

3. A fee of .0005% of payroll will be imposed on all corporations and deposited in a general relief fund for the relief of those employees whose employers fail to meet payroll.

11.8 Unemployment Insurance

Mars Colony employers must obtain unemployment insurance for their employees.

11.9 Mars Colony Government and Mars Colony Operating Company Employees

Except as otherwise provided by law, the Governor of the Mars Colony shall:

1.   appoint all officers and employees of the Mars Colony and the Mars Colony Operating Company; and

2. prescribe the compensation of officers and employees of the Mars Colony, and establish their conditions of employment, including matters related to transportation, medical care, leave, office hours and hours of labor.

3.   Compensation prescribed by the Governor under this section may not exceed, in any case, by more than 25%, the compensation paid for the same or similar work performed on Earth.

11.10 Deduction from Compensation due for Supplies or Services

Amounts due from officers and employees, whether to the Mars Colony, or MCOC, or a contractor, for transportation, board, supplies or any other service, may be deducted from the compensation otherwise payable to them, and may be paid to the authorized parties or credited to the appropriation out of which the transportation, board, supplies or other service was originally paid.

11.11 Mars Colony Operating Company Employees

1. Except as otherwise provided by law, the Company may:

2. appoint, fix the compensation of, and define the authority and duties of, officers, agents, attorneys and employees necessary for the conduct of the business of the Company;

3. delegate to the persons appointed such of its powers as it deems necessary.

4. Officers and employees of the Mars Colony may, if appointed under this section, serve as officers or employees of the Company.

11.12 Definition of Employee

For the purposes of this Code and labor within the Mars Colony, there shall be no difference drawn between permanent and temporary employees.

11.13 Labor Unions

1. An employee cannot be forced to join a labor union as a condition of employment.

2. Labor unions shall be banned from the Mars Colony for an initial period of twenty five years. At the expiration of this period, the Governor may permit the formation of labor unions following a recommendation by the Mars Colony Council.

11.14 Labor Board of Appeals

1. There is hereby established an Mars Colony Board of Labor Appeals. The Governor of the Mars Colony shall appoint three members to serve on the Board. Members so appointed shall have staggered terms. The Governor shall fix the compensation of the Board members.

2. The Board shall review and settle disputes be-

tween employers and employees under this Chapter. In addition, the Board shall adjudicate disputes between employees of license holders and license holders in the Mars Colony. The Board shall promulgate appropriate rules of procedure, and may employee investigators, attorneys and other officers it deems appropriate where necessary for the completion of its duties.

3. After investigation and consideration of the evidence submitted, the Board shall:

(a) prepare a written decision;

(b) transmit its decision to the department concerned or the parties in the case of private sector dispute;

(c)transmit copies of the decision to the employee concerned or to his designated representative.

4. The decision of the Board on any question or matter within its jurisdiction is final and conclusive.

5. Upon receipt of the Board's decision, the department or employer concerned shall take action in accordance with the decision of the Board. A license holder who fails to carry out the Board's decision shall have their license suspended until such time as the Board's decision is implemented.

6. No adverse action may be taken against an employee solely for filing a matter with the Board. An employer

who takes adverse action for this reason may be subject to fines, penalties and making the employee whole as a condition of maintaining a license in the Mars Colony.

Chapter 12

SPACEFLIGHT, TRANSPORTATION

The Governor shall prescribe, and from time to time may amend, regulations governing spacecraft, navigation facilities and spaceflight activities within the Mars Colony.

12.1 Spaceport Fees

The Company may prescribe, and from time to time change the spaceport fees that shall be imposed upon space vessels calling at the Mars Colony spaceport.

12.2 Hyperloop, Highways, Roads and Vehicles

12.2.1 Regulations

1. The Governor may make, publish and enforce, and from time to time amend, a traffic code consisting of rules and regulations for the use of the transportation corridors in the Mars Colony; and for the regulation, licensing and taxing of the use and operation of all self-propelled vehicles using the transportation corridors and roads, including but not limited to the establishment of speed limits, rules of the road, signals, tags, license fees and all detailed regulations which may, from time to time, be deemed necessary in the exercise of the authority hereby conferred.

2. The taxes on self-propelled vehicles may be graded according to their value or power.

12.3 Land Transportation

The Governor shall establish a transportation system for land transportation between the Mars Colony and its remote settlements or mining camps.

12.4 Regulations Governing Navigation, Pilotage and Licensing of Astronauts

The Governor shall prescribe, and from time to time may amend, regulations governing:

1. navigation in and around the spaceport and elsewhere as appropriate;

and

2. the licensing of astronauts or other operators of space vessels operating within the jurisdiction of the Mars Colony.

12.5 Inspection of Spacecraft

12.5.1 Vessels Subject to Inspection Generally

1. With the exception of space men of war of all nations, vessels navigating the space subject to the jurisdiction of the Mars Colony are subject to an annual safety inspection.

2. Inspections will be conducted by the Space Safety Board of Local Inspectors.

12.5.2 Issuance and Display of Certificate of Inspection

When the Space Safety Board of Local Inspectors approves a space vessel and its equipment, the Mars Colony Operating Company shall issue a certificate of inspection, in triplicate. One copy of the certificate shall be displayed in a conspicuous place on board the vessel.

12.5.3 Refusal of Certificate of Inspection

When the Space Safety Board of Local Inspectors does not approve a space vessel or its equipment, a certificate of inspection shall be refused, and the Space Safety Board of Local Inspectors shall make a statement in writing giving the reason for the refusal to approve, filing the statement in the records of the Board, with a copy thereof to the owner, agent or crew of the space vessel. A vessel with no Certificate of Inspection is not permitted to remain in navigate with Martian space and must leave at the next launch window. A space vessel unable to leave will be subject to disposal in accordance with regulations promulgated by the Governor.

12.5.4 Revocation of Certificate of Inspection

If the condition of a space vessel holding an unexpired certificate no longer conforms to the regulations under which the certificate was issued, the Space Safety Board of Local Inspectors may revoke the certificate of inspection. Upon revocation, a notice shall be issued to the owner, agent or crew of the vessel. A vessel with a revoked certificate shall make such repairs as are necessary before leaving or navigating in Martian space.

Chapter 13

PROFESSIONS AND OCCUPATIONS

13.1 Architects and Engineers

13.1.1 Practice of Architecture and Engineering as Subject to Regulation

To safeguard life, health and property and to promote the public welfare, the practice of architecture and engineering in the Mars Colony is subject to regulation in the public interest. It is further a matter of public interest and concern that the professions of architecture and engineering merit and receive the confidence of the public and that only qualified persons be permitted to engage in the practice of architecture and engineering.

13.1.2 Regulations

The Governor shall prescribe, and from time to time may amend, regulations for the Mars Colony governing the registration and practice of architects and professional engineers. The regulations may cover the:

1. issuance, suspension, revocation, and re-issuance of certificates of registration;

2. certification of architects in training and engineers in training; and

3. levying of appropriate fees.

13.2 Astronauts

1. The licensing of astronauts is subject to regulation in the public interest. It is further a matter of public interest and concern that the professions of architecture and engineering merit and receive the confidence of the public and that only qualified persons be qualified as astronauts.

2. The Mars Colony shall recognize licenses issued by any jurisdiction on Planet Earth. Astronauts regu-

larly working in the Mars Colony shall have a Planet Mars endorsement in accordance with regulations to be prescribed by the Governor.

3. The Governor shall prescribe such regulations as may be necessary for Mars-qualified astronauts.

13.3 Healing Arts

1. The Governor shall prescribe, and from time to time may amend, regulations governing the issuance of licenses to practice the healing arts, and the conditions under which the licenses may be revoked for cause.

2. Licenses issued by any jurisdiction on Planet Earth shall be recognized on Mars. As a condition of licensing in the Mars Colony, the Governor may require the completion of a localization course.

2. The practice of homeopathy is prohibited in the Mars Colony.

3. There shall be no additional penalty, sanction or liability for acts alleged to constitute medical malpractice, except where the physician is under the influence of narcotics or alcohol or where the physicians' intentional conduct is a violation of the criminal law.

4. An applicant shall pay that license fee prescribed by

the Governor.

13.4 Legal Advisors

1. The following persons may be admitted to practice law in the Mars Colony:

(a) A person who holds a license to practice law from the Mars Colony; or

(b) A person who is admitted to practice in the highest court of a sovereign nation on Planet Earth.

2. As a condition of licensing in the Mars Colony, the Governor may require the completion of a localization course.

3. The Clerk shall keep a register of persons authorized to practice before the Board. A certificate of admission shall be issued to all persons so registered.

4. An applicant for admission shall pay that fee prescribed by the Governor.

13.4.1 Attorney Trust Accounts Prohibited

1. Legal Advisors may not keep client funds.

2. Legal Advisors may establish client trust accounts to be administered by trust departments of licensed banks,

financial institutions or the Mars Colony Postal Service. Prior to disbursing funds from such accounts, the trustee shall determine, as a fiduciary, that disbursement is proper.

13.5 Injunction to Restrain Violation

The Governor may order the restraint of a person from the commission of any act prohibited by regulations established pursuant to this section.

Chapter 14

CORPORATIONS

14.1 Definition

A corporation is a legal entity created by or under the authority of the laws of the Mars Colony or a jurisdiction on Planet Earth, having a personality and existence distinct from that of its shareholders. Doing business in the Mars Colony is a privilege and not a right.

14.2 Application for License to Do Business; Service of Process; Filing Fee

A corporation organized under the laws of a sovereign nation of Planet Earth may not do business in the Mars Colony or maintain an office therein until it has filed with the Company:

1. an application for a license setting forth:

2. the name of the corporation;

3. the names of its officers and directors; and

4. the general nature of the business in which it desires to engage in the Mars Colony;

5. a copy, duly certified by the officer authorized by law to certify it, of the:

6. articles of incorporation or association;

7. charter; or

8. statutory, executive, or governmental acts creating the corporation, when it has been so created.

9. A designation of a person residing within the Mars Colony upon whom process issued under any law of the Mars Colony may be served, and his place of business or residence, and a certified copy of the board of directors of

the corporation authorizing the designation.

10. A corporation licensed pursuant to this chapter shall also file with the executive secretary or his delegate any change in the license granted or the provisions of its original articles of incorporation or association.

14.3 Additional Requirements for Insurance Companies

The Governor may prescribe additional requirements for the licensing and registration of companies which propose to underwrite risks in the Mars Colony.

14.4 Issuance of Business License

Upon compliance by a corporation with the conditions prescribed by this section, and if the Governor or his delegate is satisfied that the business desired to be transacted is proper, legitimate under the rules of the Mars Colony and not in conflict with the administration of the Mars Colony, he may issue a license to do business in the Mars Colony.

14.5 License Renewal

A license once issued may be renewed upon the payment of the appropriate fee and upon obtaining the consent of the Governor or his delegate.

14.6 Revocation or Suspension of License

The Governor or his delegate may revoke or suspend a license if, upon examination, he is satisfied that the operations of the corporation are conducted in an improper or illegal manner, or in a manner contrary to public policy, safety or the best interests of the Mars Colony in his sole discretion.

14.7 Penalties for Violation; Validity of Contracts

A corporation which does business in the Mars Colony without authorization shall be fined not more than MCU 100,000 in addition to such other penalties provided by law.

3. Every contract made by or on behalf of an unauthorized corporation affecting the liability thereof or relating to property within the Mars Colony is void on its behalf and of behalf of its assigns, but is enforceable against it or them.

14.8 Surrender of License to Do Business

1. A corporation licensed to do business in the Mars Colony may surrender its license. Such notice of surrender must contain a forwarding address and consent to service of process.

2. Corporations that have ceased operations in the Mars Colony may be sued for a period of up to five years.

3. A corporation that has ceased operations but has failed to file a formal Surrender of License notice is subject to the jurisdiction of the courts of the Mars Colony for a five year period after such notice is filed and for the duration of any proceeding commenced prior to the end of such period.

4. Mere cessation of business operations in the Mars Colony without filing a notice of surrender of license does

not revoke the appointment of any agent for the service of process within the Mars Colony.

14.9 Service of Process After Revocation or Surrender of License

1. After the license of a corporation has been revoked or surrendered, process against the corporation may be served by mail upon the executive secretary of the Mars Colony Operating Company in any action or dispute arising before the surrender or revocation of the license if the directors of the corporation no longer have a presence on Mars Colony.

2. The revocation or surrender of a license does not affect a pending action.

Chapter 15

REAL PROPERTY

1. All real property on Mars Colony is vested in the Office of the Governor.

2. Such real property may be occupied or utilized subject to a license granted by the Governor.

3. A license issued by the governor may be referred to as a "lease title."

15.1 Acquisition of Personalty or Structures

Within the limits of available funds, the Governor may:

1. purchase or otherwise acquire equipment; and

2.   within the Mars Colony, purchase or otherwise acquire, construct, repair, replace, alter, or enlarge any building, structure or other improvement—when, in his judgment, the action is necessary for the civil government, including health, sanitation and protection of the Mars Colony.

15.2 Towns, Subdivisions, Licenses to Occupy Land

The Governor of the Mars Colony shall:

1. Determine what towns or subdivisions shall be established in the Mars Colony.

2. Whenever the Governor deems it necessary and appropriate, he or his designee may issue revocable licenses covering the use of tracts of land situated within the Mars Colony.

3. The Governor shall prescribe the terms and conditions of licenses issued under this section, except that the licenses shall be revocable at the pleasure of the Governor and except that, upon revocation of a license hereunder, the licensee shall, immediately, or upon such reasonable notice as the Governor prescribes, vacate the li-

censed area, remove therefrom all improvements which he may have placed upon the licensed area, and restore the licensed area to a condition satisfactory to the Governor.

4. The licensee is not entitled to indemnification for the value of the improvements. No compensation may be paid in the case of license revoked, where the licensee has abandoned the license, or in case of the death or dissolution of the licensee.

15.3 Personal Property

15.3.1 Ownership as Absolute or Qualified

The ownership of personal property is either absolute or qualified:

1. Ownership of personal property is absolute when one person has the absolute dominion over it, and may use it or dispose of it according to his pleasure within the confines of the law.

2. Ownership is qualified when:

(a) it is shared with one or more persons;

(b) the time of enjoyment is deferred or of a limited duration, such as a lease;

(c) the use is restricted.

15.4 Rights of Owners

1. A holder of real property under a license issued by the Governor is entitled to the rents and profits deriving from that property.

2. The owner of personal property owns also dividends upon stock and other produce of personal property.

15.5 Causes of Action

1. A debt, or a cause of action in respect of a debt, is not extinguished by death.

2. An action thereon may be brought or continued by or against the personal representative of the deceased person.

15.6 Fixtures

1. When a person, such as a tenant, affixes his property to the land held under a lease issued by the Governor without an agreement permitting him to remove it, the thing

affixed belongs to the Mars Colony unless the Governor chooses to require the tenant to remove it.

2. A tenant may remove fixtures he has made, unless:

(a) the removal would cause injury to the premises; or

(b) the thing has become an integral part of the premises by the manner in which it was affixed.

Chapter 16

TRANSFER OF REAL PROPERTY LEASES (CADASTRE SYSTEM)

16.1 Definitions

1. Transfer is an act of the parties, or of the law, by which a Mars Colony lease is conveyed from one person to another.

2. A voluntary transfer is an executed contract and is subject to all rules concerning contracts.

16.2 Property which may be Transferred

Property of any kind may be transferred.

16.3 Right of Repossession as Transferable

A right of repossession for breach of condition subsequent may be transferred.

16.4 Vesting of Title

1. In the case of real property:

   (a) lease title vests upon the registration of the contract of sale in the Mars Colony cadastre system.

   2. In the case of personal property:

   (a) title vests upon transfer of possession.

16.5 Escrow

A lease title under a contract of sale may be deposited by the grantor with a third person, such as a bank, to be delivered on performance of a condition. On performance of the condition, the delivery will be made and will take effect. While in the possession of the third person, and subject to the condition, the transaction is in escrow.

Chapter 17

MARS COLONY DISPUTE RESOLUTION SYSTEM

17.1 Dispute Resolution Board

17.1.1 Establishment and Designation of Board

There is hereby established a dispute resolution committee in the Mars Colony, designated as the "Mars Colony Dispute Resolution Board".

17.1.2 Sessions of Board

Sessions of the Board shall be held at such times as the Board designates by rule or by order.

17.1.3 Appointment of Board Members

1. The Governor shall appoint board members who shall hold office for a term of five years, staggered.

2. The salary of board members shall be set in accordance with those of other Mars Colony employees according to rates established pursuant to this Code.

3. Board members shall not be removed save for misconduct.

17.1.4 Public Legal Advisor

1. When appropriate and necessary to facilitate the orderly progression of the Board's business, the Board may nominate on an ad hoc basis a qualified legal advisor to act on behalf of individuals who do not have the economic resources to afford their own counsel.

2. Legal services provided by the public legal advisor may only be rendered to individuals.

17.2 Competency, General Provisions

17.2.1 Competency, Jurisdiction

1. The Disputes Resolution Board shall resolve disputes among licensees in the Mars Colony.

2. The Labor and Minor Disputes Board shall resolve and settle minor disputes that arise among licensees and residents with a value of no more than MCU 10,000.

3. Notwithstanding any other provision of law or contract, by virtue of accepting a Mars Colony license, a licensee or resident consents to the exercise of the jurisdiction of the Mars Colony Disputes Resolution Board over those matters within the competence of the Board.

17.2.2 No Jurisdiction Over Certain Matters

The Disputes Resolution Board shall not have jurisdiction over:

1. criminal actions;

2. actions between a licensee and a non-licensee; except minor matters or to declare rights;

3. security or similar matters;

4. any other matter that the Governor decides shall not be within the jurisdiction of the Board due to health and

safety concerns.

17.2.3 Proceedings to be Public

1. The proceedings of the Board shall be public, except where the Board may direct, concerning a sensitive or appropriate matter, such as trade secrets, family relations and the like, that all persons, except Board members, Board officers and employees, the parties, their witnesses and counsel. Witnesses in a proceeding may be excluded until after they have finished giving their testimony.

2. The Board may direct the Clerk to seal the records of any case in which the proceedings or documents and records related thereto should not be made public.

17.2.4 Powers of the Board

1. The Board has the power, generally, to:

(a) preserve and enforce order in the proceedings before it;

(b) compel obedience to its judgments, orders and process;

(c) control, in the furtherance of its mission, the conduct of its ministerial officers and all other persons in any manner connected with a pending proceeding, in every matter appertaining thereto;

(d) require the attendance of persons to testify;

(e) amend and controls its process and orders so as to make them conformable to law and judgment.

2. With respect to a particular case or controversy:

(a) summon witnesses to testify in matters;

(b) administer oaths;

(c) require the production of books and records.

17.2.5 Means to Carry Jurisdiction into Effect

When jurisdiction is conferred on a Board by this Code, all the means necessary to carry it into effect are also given. In the exercise of this jurisdiction, if the course of proceeding is not specifically prescribed by this Code, any suitable process or mode of proceeding may be adopted, by rule or by a ruling in a particular case, which appears most suitable to the spirit of this Code and in the furtherance of justice.

17.2.6 Allowance of Specific or Preventive Relief

Specific or preventive relief may be given as provided by the laws applicable in the Mars Colony.

17.2.7 Method of Giving Specific Relief

1. Specific relief is given by:

(a) taking possession of a thing and giving it to a claimant;

(b) compelling a party himself to do that which ought to be done; or

(c) declaring and determining the rights of the parties, including an award of damages.

2. Method of Giving Preventive Relief

Preventive relief is by prohibiting a party from doing that which ought not to be done.

17.2.8 Specific Performance

The specific performance of an obligation may be compelled.

17.2.9 Mutuality of Remedy

Neither party to an obligation may be compelled specifically to perform it, unless the other party thereto has performed, or is compellable specifically to perform, everything to which the former is entitled under the same obligation.

17.2.10 Injunctive Relief

The Disputes Resolution Board is authorized to grant preventive relief by injunction, either temporary or final.

17.3 Enforcement

1. A licensee who fails to comply with an order of the Board shall lose his license in the Mars Colony.

2. To the extent possible, the orders and decisions of the Board shall be self-executing.

17.4 Fees and Costs

17.4.1 Each Party Responsible for His Own Costs

1. Each party to a proceeding before the Board shall be responsible for the costs incurred by him in the action.

2. The Board shall require that costs be paid before notification of the proceedings is issued.

3. The Board may waive costs in cases of substantiated indigency.

17.5 Attorneys Fees

Each party shall be responsible for the costs of his own counsel in any proceedings before the Board. The Board may not award attorneys fees to a prevailing party as an element of damages in any decision.

17.5.1 Attorneys Fees, Contingent and Success Fees Prohibited

1. An attorney is entitled to have and recover from his client reasonable compensation for the services rendered.

2. Any contract to compensate an attorney which is contingent upon the recovery of money is void.

3. Any contract to compensate an attorney based upon the outcome of the case, or as a "success fee," is void.

4. An attorney may share no financial interests with his client.

17.6 Minor Matters Board

A Minor Matters Board is hereby established as a subdivision of the Mars Colony Dispute Resolution Board to be designated as the "Mars Colony Minor Matters Disputes Board".

17.6.1 Appointment of Board Members

The Governor shall appoint those members of the Minor Matters Disputes Board as he sees fit.

17.6.2 Jurisdiction of Board; Proceedings, Operations

1. The board shall resolve and settle minor disputes with a value of no more than MCU 10,000.

2. One board member shall preside over proceedings of the Minor Matters Disputes Board.

3. There shall be no appeal from the decisions of the Minor Matters Disputes Board.

4. Parties shall not be represented by attorneys in proceedings before the Minor Matters Board.

Chapter 18

COMMERCIAL RULES

General Provisions

Construction of Title

This title establishes rules for the Mars Colony respecting the subjects to which it relates and shall be construed liberally.

18.1 Rules of Construction

The following rules of construction shall aid in the interpretation of this Code.

1. When the reason of a rule ceases, so should the rule itself.

2. Where the reason is the same, the rule should be the

same.

3. Rule to suppress the mischief and advance the remedy.

4. One may waive the advantage of a law intended for his benefit.

5. A public law cannot be contravened by a private agreement.

6. The exercise of a private right must not infringe upon the rights of others.

7. One who consents to an act is not wronged by it.

8. Acquiescence in error waives a subsequent objection.

9. One cannot take advantage of his own wrong.

10.One who has fraudulently dispossessed himself of a thing may be treated as if he still had possession.

11.One who, with knowledge, can and does not forbid that which is done on his behalf is deemed to have bidden it.

12.One should not suffer by the act of another.

13.One who takes the benefit must bear the burden.

14.For every wrong there is a remedy.

15.Between those who are equally in the right or equally in the wrong, the law does not decide.

16.Between rights otherwise equal, the first established is preferred.

17.No one is responsible for that which no one can control.

18.Rights may be extinguished by failure to exercise them.

19.The law favors substance over form.

20.That which ought to have been done is to be regarded as done, in favor of him to whom, and against him from whom, performance is due.

21.The law never requires impossibilities.

22.The law does not concern itself with trifling matters.

23.Particular expressions qualify those which are general.

24.The expression of one thing is the exclusion of another.

25.A lie about one thing implies lying about others.

26.Contemporaneous recollection is superior to subsequent reconstruction.

27.The greater contains the lesser.

28.Time does not confirm a void act.

29.A contract consists of offer and acceptance.

30.Consideration is not required for contracts in the Mars Colony.

31.A contract for an uncertain object is void.

32.Oral contracts are valid, but should be reduced to writing as soon as is practicable and in any case within thirty sols of striking agreement. The failure to reduce an agreement to writing shall be held against the party who seeks an interpretation of the contract not in harmony with his counterpart.

33.A force majeure event suspends contract performance.

34.An act to be performed on a particular sol, which falls upon a holiday or weekend, may be performed on the next business sol, with the same effect as if it had been performed on the sol appointed.

18.2 Contracts by Minors

1. Contracts entered into by minors are voidable.

2. If, before the contract of a minor is disaffirmed, the goods which he has bought or sold are transferred to another purchaser who bought them in good faith for value and without notice of the transferor's defect of title, the minor may not recover the goods from an innocent purchaser.

18.3 Contracts by Unreasoning, Unsound or Incapacitated

A person entirely without reasoning, a person of unsound mind, or a mentally incapacitated person may not make a contract.

18.4 Contracts and Sale of Goods

18.4.1 Definition

A contract is an agreement to do or not to do a certain thing.

18.5 Essential Elements of Contract

It is essential to the existence of a contract that there should be:

1. parties capable of contracting;
2. an offer; and
3. an acceptance.

Consideration is not required for the formation of a valid contract.

18.5.1 Consent

18.5.2 Essentials of Consent

The consent of the parties to a contract must be:

1. free;

2. mutual; and

3. communicated by each to the other.

18.5.3 Lack of Consent

An apparent consent is not real or free when obtained through:

1. duress, threat or menace;

2. fraud; or

3. mutual mistake

4.the presence of uncertainty.

18.6 Offers

1. An offer may be revoked at any time before its acceptance is communicated to the offeror, but not afterwards.

2. An offer is revoked by communicating the revocation to the offeree.

18.7 Acceptance

1. Performance of the conditions of an offer constitutes acceptance.

2. An acceptance which varies the terms of an offer is not an acceptance.

18.8 Object

1. The object of a contract must be lawful when the contract is made.

2. A contract whose object is unascertainable or unknowable is void.

18.9 Types of Contracts

A contract is either express or implied.

18.9.1 Express Contract

An express contract is one the terms of which are stated in words.

18.9.2 Implied Contract

An implied contract is one the existence and terms of which are manifested by conduct.

18.9.3 Oral Contracts

Contracts may be oral, but oral contracts must be committed to writing as soon as is practicable to do so.

18.10 Effect of Written Contract

The execution of a contract in writing supersedes all the negotiations or stipulations concerning its matter which preceded or accompanied the execution of the instrument.

18.11 Contract Interpretation

18.12 Intention of Parties

A contract shall be interpreted so as to give effect to the mutual intention of the parties as it existed at the time of contracting, insofar as the same is ascertainable and lawful.

18.13 Language of Contract

1. The language of a contract shall govern its interpretation, if the language is clear and explicit.

2. Where a contract has been reduced to writing, the intention of the parties shall be ascertained from the writing alone; except where a contract is in excess of forty pages in length, double spaced, twelve point type.

3. The whole of a contract shall be taken together, so as to give effect to every part, if reasonably practicable, each cause helping to interpret the other.

4. The words of a contract shall be understood in their ordinary sense, rather than according to strict legal meaning, unless used by the parties in a technical sense, or unless a special meaning is to be given to them by the usage of the parties.

5. Technical words shall be interpreted as usually understood by persons in the profession or business to which they relate, unless clearly used in a different sense.

6. Words in a contract which are wholly inconsistent with its nature, or with the intention of the parties, shall be rejected.

7. A contract may be explained by reference to the circumstances under which it was made, and the matter to

which it relates.

18.14 Writing Disregarded

When a written contract fails to express the real intention of the parties, that intention shall be regarded, and the erroneous parts of the writing disregarded.

18.15 Interpretation in Favor of Contract

A contract shall receive such an interpretation as will make it lawful, operative, definite, reasonable and capable of being carried into effect, if it can be done without violating the intention of the parties.

18.16 Partly Written and Printed Contracts

If a contract is partly written and partly printed:

1. Handwriting controls parts written by typewriter or laser printer;

2. Parts written by typewriter or produced by laser printer control the printed parts.

18.17 Interpretation against Party Causing Ambiguity

In cases of ambiguity not removed by the preceding rules, the language of a contract shall be interpreted most strongly against the party who caused the ambiguity to exist. The offeror is presumed to be that party, even if the parties agree to have written the contract jointly.

18.18 Time of Performance

If a time for performance is not specified in the contract, a reasonable time is allowed.

18.19 Contracts Contrary to Public Policy

The following contracts or contract clauses are deemed to be against public policy:

1. A contract which has as its object, either directly or indirectly, the exemption of anyone from responsibility for his own faults, or negligent injury to the person or property of another, are against public policy.

2. A clause establishing such an exemption in a contract will be disregarded, but the contract will otherwise be given effect.

18.20 Liquidated Damages

1. Liquidated damages in the nature of a fine or punishment are against public policy.

2. A clause establishing liquidated damages in the nature of a fine or punishment will be disregarded, but the contract will otherwise be given effect.

3. The parties may agree upon an amount which shall be presumed to be the amount of damage caused by a breach of contract when, from the nature of the case, it would be impracticable or extremely difficult to fix the actual damage. Such presumptive damages must be reasonable and may not be punitive in nature.

18.21 Extinction of Contracts

18.21.1 Rescission

A contract is extinguished by its rescission by mutual agreement.

18.21.2 Novation

A contract is extinguished by its novation by mutual agreement.

18.21.3 Full Performance

A contract is extinguished when fully-performed; however, confidentiality and similar provisions may nevertheless continue after the time the contract is otherwise fully performed.

18.22 Statute of Limitations in Contracts for Sale

1. Any action sought to be prosecuted before the Disputes Board must be commenced within 4 years after the cause of action has accrued. By the original agreement the par-

ties may reduce the period of limitation to not less than one year but may not extend it.

2. A cause of action accrues when the breach occurs, regardless of the aggrieved party's lack of knowledge of the breach. A breach of warranty occurs when tender of delivery is made, except that where a warranty explicitly extends to future performance of the goods and discovery of the breach must await the time of such performance the cause of action accrues when the breach is or should have been discovered.

Chapter 19

TORTS

A person may not injure the person or property of another.

19.1 Intentional Torts

Intentional torts consist of the following:

Assault;

Battery;

Conversion,

False Imprisonment;

Trespass.

Torts in the nature of the intentional infliction of emotional distress and libel and slander are not actionable.

19.2 Willful Acts and Negligence; Contributory Negligence

1. A person is responsible, not only for the result of his willful acts, but also for an injury occasioned to another by his want of ordinary care or skill in the management of his property or person, except as far as the latter has willfully brought the injury upon himself.

2. Want of ordinary care on the part of the injured person does not bar a recovery, but the damages shall be diminished by the Board in proportion to the want of ordinary care attributable to that person.

19.3 Master and Servant Liability

A Master is responsible for the torts of his servant committed in the course of his employment.

19.4 Compensation for Tort

A person who suffers a loss or harm in person or property due to the act or omission of another, may recover from the person in fault a compensation therefore in money, which is called damages.

19.4.1 Damages in Tort Cases

Damages in a tort case is the amount which will compensate for all the detriment caused thereby, whether it could have been anticipated or not, pain and suffering excluded.

Chapter 20

AGENCY

20.1 Agent and Agency Defined

An agent is one who represents another, called the principal, in dealings with third persons. Such a representation is called agency.

20.2 Requirement of Power of Attorney

No agency shall be valid without a written power of attorney setting forth the powers granted the agent.

20.3 Rights and Liabilities

An agent represents his principal for all purposes within the scope of his actual authority, and all the rights and liabilities which would accrue to the agent from transactions within that limit, if they had been entered into on his own account, accrue to the principal.

20.4 Termination

An agency is terminated:

1. in accordance with the terms of the power of attorney creating it;

2. its revocation by the principal;

3. by the death of the principal; and

4. one year after issuance of the power of attorney, unless the power of attorney is renewed in writing.

Chapter 21

MISCELLANEOUS

21.1 Health and Safety

21.1.1 Health, Sanitation and Quarantine

The Governor shall prescribe, and from time to time may amend, regulations governing matters of health, sanitation and quarantine for the Mars Colony.

21.2 Fire Prevention

21.2.1 Regulations for Fire Protection

The Governor shall prescribe, and from time to time may amend, regulations for the prevention of, and protection against, fires and other hazards in the Mars Colony.

21.3 Contraband

The importation or possession of contraband within the Mars Colony is subject to reasonable rules and restrictions issued from time to time by the Governor.

The Governor shall issue circulars from time to time identifying which items are deleterious to the Mars Colony, its residents and its operations.

Possession or importation of contraband in violation of this section shall be subject to fines and/or imprisonment based on nature of the item and the harm caused thereby.

The abuse of alcohol or narcotics is deemed to be a matter of public health and will be dealt with under the Mars Colony Public Health System.

21.3.1 Customs Service

The Governor has control, for customs purposes, over all articles introduced into the Mars Colony, including passengers' baggage, and shall establish, and from time to time may amend, regulations governing the:

1. entry and importation of goods into the Mars Colony; and

2. disposition of goods brought into the Mars Colony in violation of the regulations.

21.3.2 Customs Fees

A customs officer may collect those official fees prescribed from time to time by the Governor. a fee, whenever he:

1. certifies an invoice;

2. register a marine note of protest;

3. performs any notarial service.

21.4 Zoning Regulations

The Governor shall prescribe, and from time to time may amend, regulations:

1. designed to abate or prevent nuisances in the Mars Colony;

2. No live animal may be imported without the express permission of the Governor after review by the Mars Colony ecological authorities.

21.4.1 Nuisances

21.4.2 Nuisance Defined

Anything is a nuisance which:

1. is injurious to health; or

2. is indecent or offensive; or

3. is an obstruction to the free use of property, so as to interfere with the comfortable enjoyment of life or property, or

4. unlawfully obstructs the free passage or use, in the customary manner, of navigable or public space, a public park, square or highway.

21.4.3 Public Nuisance Defined

A public nuisance is one which affects at the same time an entire community or sector, or a considerable number of persons, although the extent of the annoyance or damage inflicted upon individuals may be unequal.

21.4.4 Private Nuisance Defined

A nuisance which is not a public one is a private one.

21.4.5 Abatement

The Governor may abate any nuisance, public or private.

21.5 Access to Records

21.5.1 Inspection

1. Every person having a legitimate interest therein, has the right to inspect and take a copy of any public writing or record of the Mars Colony.

2. Attorneys may examine court records and records of administrative bodies, such as the Labor Board of Appeals, the Disputes Board and the Board of Local Inspectors without the necessity of showing a legitimate interest therein.

3. Journalists may examine court records and records of administrative bodies, such as the Labor Board of Appeals, the Disputes Board and the Board of Local Inspectors without the necessity of showing a legitimate interest therein.

4. For the purpose of this subchapter, a "journalist" is any individual who regularly posts original content through any medium whatsoever, whether or not for profit.

21.5.2 Public Officers must give Copies

1. Every public officer having the custody of a public writing or record that a person has the right to inspect under this title must give him, upon demand, a certified copy of it.

2. The Governor may prescribe an appropriate fee for access to and copies of records.

About the Compiler

Michael O'Kane was the last lawyer admitted to practice in the Panama Canal Zone. While he was also admitted to practice in the American states of Illinois, Florida and Louisiana, during most of his professional life he worked overseas in Latin America, Asia and the Middle East. In 2008 he led a team that worked on a project to develop a set of laws for the governance of an autonomous region in Saudi Arabia.